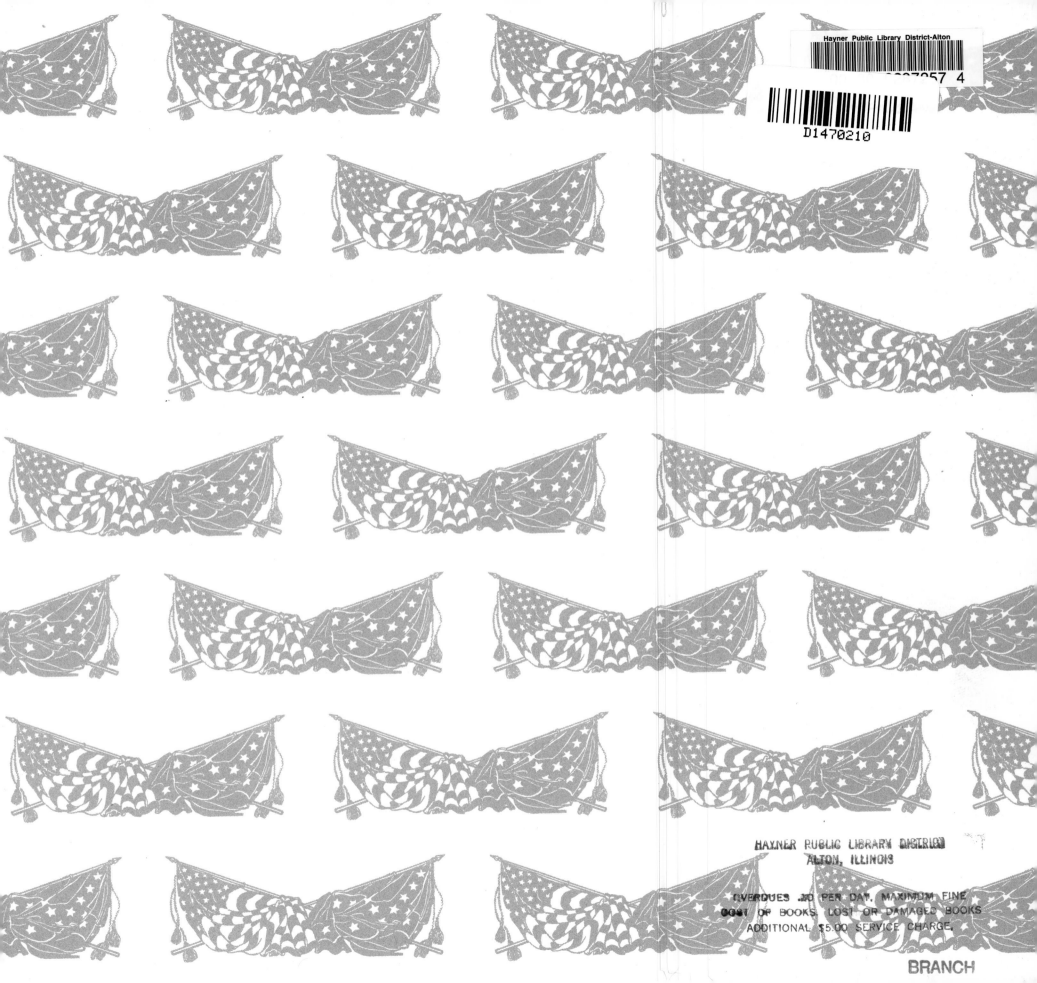

BATTLES
OF THE CIVIL WAR

William C. Davis

Designed by Philip Clucas
Featuring the Photography of Tria Giovan

2737 Battles of the Civil War
This edition published 1999 by CLB
an imprint of Quadrillion Publishing Ltd
Godalming, Surrey GU7 1XW, UK
© 1993 Quadrillion Publishing Ltd.

Distributed in the US by Quadrillion Publishing, Inc.
230 Fifth Avenue
New York 10001
Printed and bound in Singapore
All rights reserved
ISBN 1-84100-278-X

CLB

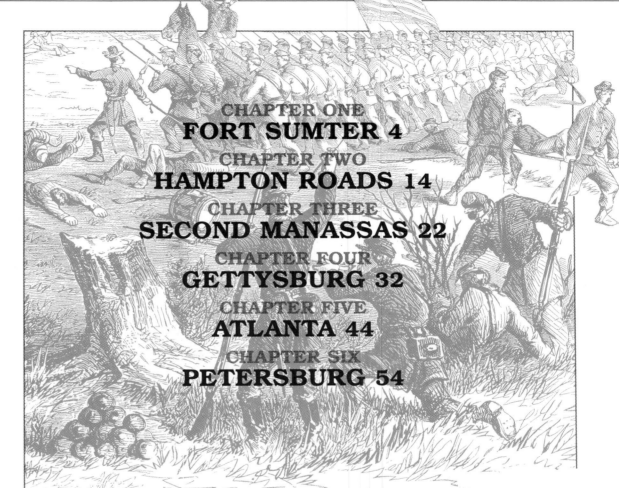

INTRODUCTION

There were more than 10,000 fights, from the greatest of battles, like Gettysburg, to the completely forgotten little skirmishes at places such as Jones' Hay Station, Arkansas. Few can agree on what constitutes exactly the first engagement. Shots were fired in obscure places even before the guns first opened in earnest at Fort Sumter; opinions divide on just when and where the last shots were fired, as well, especially since the Confederate commerce raider CSS *Shenandoah* continued to capture Yankee merchant vessels for almost six months after the Rebel armies surrendered.

But no one disputes that of all the elements that made up the American Civil War – political, social, economic, and more – it was the battles that most captured the attention and imagination of the people North and South, then and now. It was the ultimate test, the arena where history's decisions came down to epic clashes between the mightiest armies ever seen on the continent, and to the intensely personal micro-battles of one man against another. More than this, there was an incredible variety in them, from attacks on massive stationary fortresses, to open field battles, to sieges, and even epic duels between ironclad warships on the waters. Every one was different. In every one, the blood, determination, and heroism were the same.

LEFT: A romantic lithograph depicting sword-wielding General Phil Sheridan leading his men into battle at Cedar Creek, in 1864. It was the kind of idealized picture of war that was soon belied by the real horrors.

CHAPTER ONE

FORT SUMTER

In the decades following the winning of its independence, the United States commenced construction of a chain of large masonry forts guarding each of the harbors and river mouths along its Atlantic and Gulf coastlines. Each was designed to defend against attack from seaward; no one conceived that they might, instead, be attacked from the land, from the rear, and by fellow Americans. Many of these forts were situated in Southern states, and when secession led first South Carolina, and then the other states, to pass ordinances of secession in 1860-61, these forts and their Federal garrisons immediately became bones of contention.

Confederates claimed the forts as rightfully their own, and wanted the Yankee soldiers withdrawn immediately. Several, barely manned at all, yielded without a fight. But there was one that would not.

Fort Sumter sat on an artificial island of rubble in the middle of Charleston harbor, staring in the face the South Carolina city that had always been the seedbed of secession sentiment, and where the first secession ordinance was passed in December 1860. The fort was largely unfinished as yet, with many of its guns not yet mounted on their parapets, the barracks incomplete, and some of the brick casemates still lacking their hardware and fittings.

4

FACING PAGE: Major Robert Anderson was truly a man caught in the middle, between his Southern sympathies, and his firm duty to his uniform. No one felt the tragedy of Fort Sumter more than he. LEFT: Others were delighted at the coming of war, none more so than the vitriolic old secessionist Edmund Ruffin, emblematic of the kind of fanaticism on both sides that brought on the war.

ABOVE: Opportunists like Louis T. Wigfall of Texas, mixed conflicting and often ill-defined personal motives into their support for secession, and war. They all lived to regret the curse they brought on the land.

When South Carolina seceded, the fort was not yet manned, the Federal garrison in Charleston occupying Fort Moultrie and other works on the mainland. Major Robert Anderson, a Kentuckian and a slave-holder, commanded the tiny garrison of just 87 officers and men, including musicians, and as demands for turning over the fort increased in late December after the secession declaration, he feared for his exposed position in Moultrie. While negotiations fumbled on between South Carolina and Washington, he took action on his own.

On the night of Christmas, 1860, Anderson spiked the guns at Moultrie and secretly rowed his small command out to Fort Sumter. There, at least, he would not be susceptible to assault by the Confederate militia even then gathering around Charleston. His act outraged the South Carolinians, who accused him of committing a hostile act, and now there were renewed demands for the surrender

ABOVE: Within only two days of the fall of Fort Sumter, gloating Confederates were bringing cameras into the ruins to capture the scene of the fort and its conquerors. Here on the terre plain and parapet of the eastern face of the fort can be seen evidence of some of the damage done, along with two of the cannon that Anderson managed to use sporadically to return fire.

RIGHT: A youthful South Carolinian poses calmly inside the dreaded "Ironclad Battery" that had done quite a bit to wreak some of that destruction on Fort Sumter. It was from this interior that the famed old secessionist Edmund Ruffin had fired one of the first shots of the war. As irony would have it Ruffin would also fire one of the last, a bullet into his own brain in 1865, when he could not face the fact of Southern defeat. It was such extremism on both sides that had brought on the war.

of Sumter. Instead, Anderson feverishly worked to make a few of its cannon operational and get its defenses in order. For the next three-and-a-half months Anderson held out, and the Confederates held their fire. Washington tried in January to send a relief expedition by sea, but the Southerners scared the ships away. In April another supply fleet was sent, due to arrive on the twelfth.

The Confederates knew it was coming. Colonel P.G.T. Beauregard had been sent to take command in Charleston, and, with orders from the new Confederate government not to allow Sumter to be resupplied, he sent officers of his staff out to see Anderson on the afternoon of April 11. They issued another demand for surrender. Anderson refused, but hinted that he might be starved out in a few

ABOVE: As soon as the news of Sumter's fall spread, fanciful depictions of the bombardment erupted from presses around the divided nation. Few were accurate, but almost all made it look glorious – and clean.

7

ABOVE: More of the victors, some in civilian attire, cluster outside the sally port of the fallen fortress. It quickly became the most popular tourist spot in the South.

RIGHT: Dignitaries including governors and future generals like Wade Hampton, in the tall hat at center, inspected the fort's ruins and pronounced the achievement of its taking wonderful.

FACING PAGE: Certainly the damage done was something new in their experience, for such cannon as those used had never been fired in anger before on the continent. But Sumter would be ruined far more than this before war's end.

days anyhow without relief. Beauregard sent back another mission just after midnight, inquiring exactly when Anderson would have to leave or starve. The major said he would leave by noon on April 15 "should I not receive … additional supplies." Knowing that the relief ships could arrive at any hour, Beauregard decided this was not good enough.

At 4:30 a.m. on April 12, 1861, the boom of a cannon echoed across the harbor, and Anderson and his men saw a sputtering shell arch high into the heavens, exploding almost directly over them. It was the signal shell to open the bombardment, and within seconds almost fifty cannon and mortars belched forth a hail of iron that, once commenced, went on continuously for the next thirty-three hours. In that time, some 3,341 cannon balls and shells would be fired at the fort, from batteries that ringed the harbor and surrounded the beleaguered Federals.

ABOVE: Charleston photographer George S. Cook took his camera into Sumter months before the bombardment to take portraits of Major Anderson and his officers. The major's calm visage belies the turmoil he was enduring inside. With typical wit for the time, Cook published his photos with the pun "Major Anderson Taken."

ABOVE: Confederate artist Conrad Wise Chapman's excellent 1863 painting of the interior of one of the gun tiers of Fort Sumter shows it much as it would have looked in 1861, the only difference being that no such tranquil scene of a gunner asleep beside his piece would have been likely. The din inside the casemates was terrible, the atmosphere choking from the acrid gunsmoke. When these mighty columbiads fired they created a concussion like an earthquake. No one slept during the day on April 12-14, 1861.

In response, Anderson had only twenty-one guns on the fort's lower casemate tier, most of them 32-pounder smoothbores. When the first Confederate shots began to strike the fort, he held his own fire. After all, there was little damage that he could do, and he hesitated to shoot back. No war had actually been declared, but making a real battle of this might lead to it. And he would not uselessly expose his men.

Morning came and went. The garrison ate their meager breakfast of fat pork and water. Only after several hours under bombardment did he form the men on the parade and give them orders. They would work a limited number of the guns in the protected casemates. There was little they could do other than maintain their honor by refusing meekly to sit idle and take a pounding.

The first Yankee shot was fired by Major Abner Doubleday, a man often erroneously credited with inventing the game of baseball. When the Confederates heard the report of his 32-pounder, they actually cheered, as they would do so from time to time for the rest of the day. They cheered in admiration of the plucky Yankees fighting back, and they cheered that their inevitable victory would not be cheapened by being unresisted.

As the hours of bombardment dragged on, the Rebels' fire became increasingly accurate, and their shot started to turn the interior of the fort into rubble. Meanwhile, the answering fire from the fort did almost no damage at all, so well were the Confederate batteries protected. After midday the wooden barracks inside Sumter caught fire, and soon burned out of control. Flying masonry also

wounded four of Anderson's soldiers. By noon Anderson also found that his supply of powder bags for charging the guns was running low, and he had to reduce firing to just six guns. Even those he silenced at nightfall. The only good news that evening was a downpour that put out the fire in the barracks. But that hardly made up for the sight of the relief fleet, which had come in sight outside the harbor that afternoon, but which declined to risk

ABOVE: Abner Doubleday happily fired the first return shot, stirred to a vengeful mood by the destruction taking place inside and outside the walls of Fort Sumter. TOP LEFT: The shattered soldiers' quarters by the parade. BOTTOM LEFT: The sally port.

the fire of Confederate guns by coming to the fort's assistance. Anderson and his men were on their own.

Rebel shells came every fifteen minutes through the night, to keep the garrison awake. The bombardment resumed in full at dawn, but Anderson could now fire only one gun every five minutes in response. The barracks took fire again, dangerously close to the powder magazine. Sumter filled with smoke and flames, and the Yankees faced the possibility of roasting or suffocation. Once again the Confederates cheered their foemen's bravery in continuing to resist. Then a shot brought down Sumter's flag, and Confederates thought that Anderson might be surrendering. Emissaries rowed out to the fort, and even though Anderson had not

intended to yield, negotiations resulted in his agreeing to evacuate the following day. At 1:30 p.m. on April 14, the bombardment stopped.

The next day, at 2:0 p.m., Major Anderson officially turned over the fort, only after firing an intended hundred-gun salute to his flag as he took it down. Tragically, an accident during the firing led to the death of a private, and cut short the salute at fifty. Two hours later, after burying Private Daniel Hough, the first man killed in the Civil War, Anderson marched out of the fort and put his men aboard transports for the trip North. As he left, he carried under his arm his beloved flag. Four years later to the day, with the war all but over, Anderson would come back to Fort Sumter and raise that same flag once more.

FACING PAGE: The officers' quarters are equally as ruined as the enlisted men's, and on the parade in front the remains of the flagstaff pays tribute to the fire directed against it. ABOVE: Young Confederates form a rough line on the parade, many of them recent arrivals judging from the knapsacks and blanket rolls on their backs. There is a long war ahead of them.

CHAPTER TWO

HAMPTON ROADS

Following Sumter's fall, North and South mobilized for battle, more states seceded to join the Confederacy, and America went to war. The first real land battle came in July, at Bull Run in Virginia, with more fights out in Missouri that fall. President Lincoln imposed a blockade of Southern ports to prevent assistance reaching the Rebels from abroad, and early in 1862 movements began to retake the Mississippi Valley from the Confederates. Federal troops were also poised to march on the new enemy capital at Richmond, Virginia, moving from a base at Fort Monroe, beside Hampton Roads, a fort that managed to remain in Yankee hands. Such a thrust from below and east

Symbols of the hopeful
Confederate Navy.
TOP: The ironclad CSS *Virginia* in a
fanciful artist's rendition.
ABOVE: The Navy Department seal.

of Richmond might be deadly effective, but it depended upon troops and supplies being brought to Fort Monroe by water from the North, and if the Rebels could break the blockade and deny access to Hampton Roads, such a thrust could be thwarted.

Almost from the first, in April 1861, when Lincoln declared the blockade, Confederates turned their minds to ways of breaking it. If Rebel ships could get through or, better yet, if Federal ships could be driven off or destroyed, then European shipping could reach Southern ports and major powers might declare the blockade ineffective, and therefore illegal.

But, as with everything else, the South had too

few warships, really only those captured at the outset when shipyards on its coastline were seized. Worse, facilities for building new vessels were almost nonexistent. The best Confederate hope was in converting vessels to its purpose, and here the new nation encountered a stroke of good fortune.

When Virginia seceded, Confederates quickly overran Federal installations in the Old Dominion. They took the Navy Yard at Norfolk and Portsmouth, and even though the evacuating Yankees attempted to destroy everything left behind, they were too hasty at their work. Machinery was still usable. Better yet, ships set afire were not entirely destroyed, especially the huge steam frigate USS *Merrimack*. She burned only to the deck line, then was scuttled. Feverishly the Confederates raised her, refitted her machinery, and then began constructing the war's first ironclad. They fitted a massive iron ram to her prow below the waterline, mounted ten heavy naval cannon on her deck, and erected a long, sloping casemate over the guns, covering it with several inches of laminated iron sheathing.

ABOVE: The *Virginia* did not ride with her deck awash as suggested here, but she was rakishly low in the water, and her real danger lay in the iron ram on her prow, just beneath the waterline. In this colorful, though largely inaccurate, print she drives that ram into the hold of the USS *Cumberland.*

TOP: Fort Monroe played silent witness to the dramatic events of March 8-9. ABOVE: Catesby Jones assumed command of the *Virginia* when Buchanan was wounded.
RIGHT: Buchanan's brother J. McKean Buchanan was a lieutenant commander in the Yankee fleet that he attacked. Happily, both survived such sibling rivalry.

The plan was simple. Such a vessel, able to withstand anything the enemy could shoot at it, would steam out into the blockading fleet in Hampton Roads and either ram and sink Yankee wooden warships, or else blast them with her guns from the impervious security of the ironclad casemate. They called her the CSS *Virginia*. She was ready by March 8, 1862.

Early that morning Commodore Franklin Buchanan and his executive officer Lieutenant Catesby Jones got steam up in the *Virginia* and set out into Hampton Roads. Awaiting them was the Union fleet, chiefly the sloop *Cumberland* and the frigates *Congress* and *Minnesota*. The lumbering *Virginia* looked to the waiting Federals like "the roof of a barn belching forth smoke" as she approached, but they did not scoff for long. Her blazing guns almost destroyed the fleet. By the end of the day the *Minnesota* had run aground attempting to get away from her, the *Cumberland* had gone to the bottom, and the *Congress* was a blazing hulk. The Confederate ironclad had suffered

only the loss of her prow, and a painful leg wound for Buchanan. The next day she expected to go out and finish the *Minnesota* and any other Yankee ships in her path.

On the morning of March 9, as the *Virginia* steamed into Hampton Roads once more, her men saw in the distance a new ship that had arrived during the night. She looked like a "cheese box on a raft," thought one. She was the USS *Monitor*. The Confederates had not been the only ironclad

builders. When word of the terrible new vessel being constructed at Portsmouth reached Washington, Union naval leaders immediately commenced work on several ironclad designs of their own, in order to counter the *Virginia*. Swedish inventor John Ericsson submitted a design that called for a sleek, low hull, gliding barely above the water, with nothing projecting from it but a pilot house, smoke stacks, and a huge iron turret protecting two 11-inch smoothbore cannon, each of which could fire a solid

ABOVE: The mighty USS *Minnesota* very nearly became a casualty of the *Virginia's* blazing guns when she ran aground in Hampton Roads. Only the end of the day saved her from receiving the full attention of the Rebel monster, which steamed into the Roads again the next day expecting to have an easy time of finishing her off.

shot weighing 168 pounds. After each firing, the turret could be revolved away from the enemy to allow reloading of the guns in safety. In one of history's closest bits of timing, she was ready just as the *Virginia* was being completed, and hurried to Hampton Roads just in time.

Naval observers North and South watched anxiously to see the meeting of the two iron leviathans. At about eight a.m. the moment came. Deciding to ignore the little *Monitor*, the *Virginia* made for the helpless *Minnesota*. But then the Yankee ironclad steamed out to place herself in the way, and quickly the contest became one of iron against iron. For maneuverability, the *Monitor* had the best of it from the first. She was lighter, faster, and more agile, while the lumbering Confederate behemoth seemingly took forever to turn, and could only bring her guns to bear when turned in just the proper position, while the foe's revolving turret, though only placing two guns in opposition to ten, could fire from almost any position.

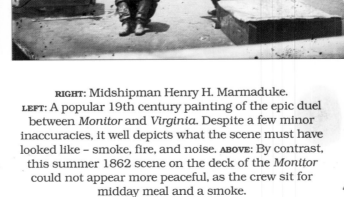

RIGHT: Midshipman Henry H. Marmaduke.
LEFT: A popular 19th century painting of the epic duel between *Monitor* and *Virginia*. Despite a few minor inaccuracies, it well depicts what the scene must have looked like – smoke, fire, and noise. ABOVE: By contrast, this summer 1862 scene on the deck of the *Monitor* could not appear more peaceful, as the crew sit for midday meal and a smoke.

For the next two hours they gave each other undivided attention. The two vessels steamed round and round each other, firing almost constantly. The *Virginia* got marginally the worst of it from the beginning, the enemy's shells cracking and knocking loose several of the iron plates protecting the

TOP: Unfortunately, no overall photograph exists that shows the entire *Monitor*. This picture was taken in the summer of 1862, showing the turret as it still evidences the effects of some of the *Virginia's* shot. The sloping roof of the new pilothouse appears in the distance.

FAR RIGHT: Lieutenant John Worden was commanding his first ship when he took over the *Monitor*, and the March 9 engagement was the only one in which he would do so, being wounded late in the day while in his pilothouse.

RIGHT: Midshipman Hardin B. Littlepage was one of those on the *Virginia* firing guns at Worden. Most of them were young, and very brave.

casemate. Had Lieutenant John Worden been able to concentrate his fire against a particular point on the Rebel ironclad, he might have broken through. If so, then one exploding shell inside the casemate would most likely have put the *Virginia* out of action.

Meanwhile, aboard the *Monitor* there were problems, too. The machinery controlling the revolving turret was clumsy and hard to operate. Finally the gunners just let the turret keep turning, and fired their guns "on the fly" as the enemy turned into view through the gun ports. The Confederate shells did the turret no real harm,

causing only dents, but occasionally an impact knocked loose a bolt head inside the turret, turning it into a deadly missile that shot across the interior.

The *Virginia* tried to ram the *Monitor*, not knowing yet of the missing ram, but moved so slowly that the ships only glanced off each other harmlessly. Finally the *Monitor* pulled away when a chance shot struck the pilot house and blinded Worden. His executive Lieutenant, Samuel D. Greene, took command, but when he turned back to resume the contest, he saw the *Virginia* steaming back to Portsmouth. Each vessel thought the other had given up.

The battle itself was inconclusive, though the blockade remained in effect and the *Virginia* never again did battle with Union ships. Two months later her own crew destroyed her when Norfolk was recaptured by the Federals. The *Monitor* fought again on the James River, but ineffectively, and finally sank in a storm that December off North Carolina. But they had started something, these vessels. "Ironclad fever" swept North and South, and scores of new monsters were laid down, inaugurating the modern era of naval warfare, and putting an end forever to the days of iron men in wooden ships.

ABOVE: In the summer of 1862, the officers of the *Monitor* sat for a cameraman, posing before the turret that had shielded them and their guns in the epic battle. Lieutenant Samuel D. Greene, who assumed command after Worden's wounding, sits on the chair at left. Some of the others are new transfers who did not participate in the battle.

CHAPTER THREE
SECOND MANASSAS

The Union lost its bid to take Richmond in the spring of 1862. Despite stopping the *Virginia*, Union operations on the Peninsula below Richmond stalled. Worse, General Thomas J. "Stonewall" Jackson's Confederates defeated three separate armies in Virginia's Shenandoah Valley. Washington itself began to fear that Rebel soldiers would be seen at its gates, and President Lincoln hastily called a new commander to assemble a new army from the fragments left and protect the Capital.

He summoned General John Pope, a flamboyant, egotistical officer who had enjoyed some limited success on the Mississippi. He was to put together

ABOVE: Major General John Pope was cursed by his own ego, McClellan's petulance, and Robert E. Lee. FACING PAGE: Here on the crest of Henry Hill at Second Manassas they all defeated him.

the new Army of Virginia, and with it march south to threaten Lee's rear while he faced the Army of the Potomac under George B. McClellan, still on the Peninsula.

Multiple misfortunes ensued. Pope offended almost everyone, especially his own officers and men, by his conceit and boastfulness. Then Lee soundly defeated McClellan on the Peninsula, but the Army of the Potomac did not leave, only settling down for the summer, while a petulant McClellan did nothing to hold Lee in place, and also refused to send any of his own men to reinforce Pope. Still, Pope would have three corps, totaling 38,000 men, commanded by Generals Franz Sigel, Nathaniel

RIGHT: The man who gave Union commanders headaches, General Robert E. Lee conducted his first offensive at Second Manassas. ABOVE: A March 1862 photograph of the earthwork defenses erected around Manassas Junction, some of them put up by the Confederates, and then used by the occupying Federals until Jackson came to call. FACING PAGE: More fortifications left by the Rebels, and adapted by the Yankees, here men of the 13th Massachusetts. All too soon they would be fighting not for Manassas, but for their lives. TOP LEFT (inset): The house used as headquarters by Generals Pope and McDowell near Cedar Mountain. TOP CENTER (inset): A few of the casualties of Cedar Mountain.
TOP RIGHT (inset): More of Manassas before Jackson.

Banks, and Irvin McDowell – all three just a step above incompetents.

Against them would be the great Lee, fresh from his victories against McClellan. Almost disdainfully he divided his army in Richmond, right in the face of McClellan. He sent Jackson with 24,000 to central Virginia when Pope's new army advanced to the Rappahannock River, and soon afterward received the great news that Jackson had struck again, catching Banks and 8,000 Yankees isolated from the rest of their army and taking them by surprise. The Battle of Cedar Mountain, on August 9, was a Federal disaster. Worse, despite orders to leave the

Peninsula and join with Pope, McClellan did not start to move at last until August 13. Meanwhile, Pope could do nothing but stay where he was in central Virginia, between Lee and Washington, and wait for McClellan to arrive. McClellan would never arrive. Lee would get to Pope first. By mid-August, the Federal Army of Virginia numbered more than 75,000, thanks to additional reinforcements, but Lee had some 55,000 on their way to rendezvous against them. Being outnumbered never frightened

LEFT: Stonewall Jackson's lightning raid on Manassas Junction, Pope's chief supply base, struck a devastating blow to the Federals. Scenes like this one of a ruined locomotive were spread all across the Manassas plain in Jackson's wake. Cut the railroads, and you cut the flow of food, men, and weapons.

Lee. Instead, he thought only of the offensive, and now he planned a bold move to send Jackson and 24,000 men on a wide move around Pope to hit his rear, while General James Longstreet, commanding the balance of the Army of Northern Virginia, would occupy Pope's attention in his front.

Jackson struck with devastating effectiveness. He moved around Pope's flank and arrived at Manassas Junction, an important rail center near the site of the war's first battle just over a year before. Manassas was Pope's supply base, and Jackson hit and destroyed it completely. Pope had no choice but to pull back from the Rappahannock to Manassas, in order to reestablish his

ABOVE: Nothing was so calculated to crush the spirit and optimism of the men in an army as the sight of their supply base in ruins, their stockpiles of stores and ammunition destroyed, and their link with succor and safety broken. Destroy a supply base, and half the job of defeating an army was accomplished, as Jackson and Lee knew better than any others.

RIGHT: A dozen Federals lounge in the summer heat near Blackburn's Ford, on Bull Run, on July 4, 1862. It is a national holiday for them, but in a few weeks they would fight for their lives on these fields.

ABOVE: One of the most unsatisfactory generals of the entire war was the German Franz Sigel. Influential, egotistical, and utterly incompetent, he also lacked courage on more than one occasion. At Second Manassas he added no luster to his reputation.

communications with Washington. Meanwhile, Jackson's job now was to hold Pope at Manassas long enough for Lee and Longstreet to catch up. Then the two wings of the Rebel army could try to crush him between them.

Ironically, Pope thought that it was he who had Jackson trapped! He hurried his army toward Manassas, telling his men that "we shall bag the whole crowd." But his officers let him down, especially one or two loyal to McClellan, who would later be accused of intentionally dragging their feet. And then Jackson struck part of McDowell's corps in a devastating surprise attack near Groveton on the evening of August 28. The Yankees lost a third of their number, and had no choice but to retire a few miles to Manassas, where the main body of Pope's army gathered.

The Battle of Second Manassas began the next morning, August 29, and nothing worked out as

John Pope had hoped or expected. Deludedly thinking that the fight at Groveton had stopped Jackson in a vulnerable spot, Pope awoke believing that McDowell's corps would be in a position to swoop down on Stonewall and deliver a telling flank attack of its own. But McDowell was nowhere near where he was supposed to be, his command being scattered badly. Worse, Lee was only a few hours away as dawn approached, and moving fast.

The first shots were fired just after 5.30 a.m., when Sigel moved his command forward. Pope's army was spread out roughly along the old lines occupied by the Confederate army at the end of the first battle here on July 21, 1861. Ironically, the Confederates were occupying much the same position as that held by the attacking Federals in that first battle. Now Pope ordered Sigel to go forward, across the Warrenton Turnpike at Groveton, to strike Jackson's flank along an unfinished

railroad. Stonewall's men turned him back bloodily by late morning, and Sigel, ever timid, was already at the point of pulling back when his men saw a large body of Confederates approaching their exposed right flank on the turnpike. Lee and Longstreet had arrived.

Their arrival could not have been better timed or placed. Indeed, the Confederates won the first Manassas fight chiefly because of chance arrivals of fresh troops at precisely the right moment, and now history repeated itself, almost precisely on the same spot. But it took time for Lee and Longstreet to get on the field and set up their attack. Meanwhile, Pope occupied himself well into the afternoon with repeated attacks on Jackson in the railroad cut, to no avail. Pope expected McDowell and others to march around his left to take Jackson in flank, but they moved slowly and Pope waited in vain to hear the sounds of their striking Jackson. They never

ABOVE: The quiet, dusty, main street of Centreville, Virginia, presented much the same face as a hundred other Virginia villages. Yet the road running through it made the village important to the invasion or defense of northern Virginia. Though no battles were fought in its streets, battles were largely planned around control of the hamlet, and it figured prominently in two battles for Manassas.

LEFT: In March 1862 photographers came to Bull Run to record the ruins of the Stone Bridge on the Centreville-Warrenton pike, and the waters of Bull Run, soon to run red with blood once more.

did. Receiving word of Lee's arrival, McDowell stayed put until nightfall.

When the battle resumed the next day, Pope still believed he had the upper hand tactically, but his army was in a bad way for supplies, and no help was forthcoming from McClellan, who by now was back in Washington. Still, he believed that he had only Jackson facing him, and then by noon actually changed his mind to assert that the Confederates were now retreating! In fact, Pope was all along making erroneous deductions from misinterpreted intelligence, and did not get his attack going until about 3:00 p.m., giving Lee all the time he needed to rest his troops and make his plans.

Pope's renewed attack on the railroad cut was vicious, but Jackson's men repulsed assault after assault. Then McDowell, in immediate command, foolishly called for a division from the left flank, south of the Warrenton Turnpike, even though

reports were now coming in of a large enemy presence – Longstreet – in that area. As soon as the division had moved, Longstreet and half Lee's army struck. The effect was electric. The Confederates drove everything before them as the Federals, hit in the flank and rear, fell back almost in panic. Longstreet started to wheel his line to the left, like a book closing, with his own line the right half, and Jackson's the left, and the Yankees in the middle.

By late afternoon Pope had to admit that he was beaten. From there on it was a scramble to save his army. He had lost 14,500 killed, wounded, and captured, out of his 70,000-man army; Lee lost 9,400 of his 55,000. Three days later the campaign was over, Pope was defeated, the Union was in a panic, and Lee was ready to march into Maryland in his first invasion of the North. Twice witness to humiliating defeats for the North, Manassas would be an ill omen for Yankees for the rest of the war.

FACING PAGE: Men started erecting monuments even while the war raged. One of the very first was this red sandstone pyramid on Henry Hill, raised in memory of men who fell in the August 1862 battle and dedicated in June 1865, when hostile Confederates were still in the field in a few places. ABOVE: The countryside around Centreville was turned into successive armed camps by both Blue and Gray. In March 1862 it looked like this after the Rebels evacuated. The Federals used much the same earthworks that summer, but never had to fight to defend them.

CHAPTER FOUR

GETTYSBURG

The ten months following Second Manassas were not good ones for the Union in the east. Lee's invasion of Maryland was turned back at Antietam by a timorous McClellan, who might have destroyed him had he the courage. But then at Fredericksburg in December, Lee delivered a costly defeat on the Rappahannock, and the following May, at nearby Chancellorsville, he made a shambles of several army corps, though at the cost of the loss of Stonewall Jackson. Out in the west the war went better, with control of the Mississippi gradually falling to the North. Still, all eyes were on the Army of the Potomac and the Army of Northern Virginia. And all asked

Gettysburg was the widowmaker. The Reb (top) in Devil's Den, the men of the III Corps and their officers (above), and gunners like the 5th U.S. Artillery (facing page), were savaged.

the same question. Could Lee ever be beaten? One man asking the question was General George G. Meade. He was placed in command of the Army of the Potomac at a crucial moment, on June 27, 1863. It was crucial because Lee was invading the North again, trying to take the war to the enemy and relieve the pressure on Virginia. He swept up through Maryland and into Pennsylvania, stealing a march on the Federals and leaving them racing to catch up with him and at the same time keep themselves between Lee and Washington. The pressure had been too much for Joseph Hooker, the discredited commander so badly beaten at Chancellorsville. He resigned without warning, and

Lincoln gave the command to Meade without even consulting him. No commander ever faced a greater challenge. Four days after assuming command, Meade would be fighting the greatest battle in the history of the hemisphere.

Lee was driving toward the Susquehanna River, and Pennsylvania's capital at Harrisburg. Meade had to prevent that, and drove hard to catch up to the Rebels. As fortune would have it, most of the major roads leading from several points in northern Maryland and central Pennsylvania converged at

TOP RIGHT: Brigadier General Alexander Hays was one of the many middle level commanders who performed admirably at Gettysburg. **ABOVE:** A. R. Waud's sketch of the fighting on the second day of the battle.
RIGHT: George A. Custer, his bright future before him, was with the cavalry at Gettysburg.
LEFT: An 1880s lithograph of the July 3 fighting.

the modest crossroads town of Gettysburg, thirty miles southeast of Harrisburg. Meade was approaching from the south, just as Lee, trying to concentrate his scattered columns, had elements of his I and III Corps moving toward the town. Neither general planned anything to take place there. Indeed, Meade expected that the coming battle would take place several miles distant, near a place called Pipe Creek. But on the morning of July 1, advance elements of General A.P. Hill's III Corps Rebels bumped into pickets from a Yankee cavalry brigade. With alarming rapidity the skirmish mushroomed into a major battle.

Both Lee and Meade realized that Gettysburg was a strategic crossroads and needed to be held. Each general, though many miles distant, began to rush troops toward the growing engagement. That first day, the advantage lay almost entirely with the Confederates. The Yankees were badly outnumbered, and tried only to fight a holding action until more help arrived. General John Reynolds strove bravely to maintain a defensive line, but then a marksman's bullet cut him down. Command devolved upon his next in line, General Abner Doubleday, the same man who fired the first Yankee shot at Fort Sumter. He was soon superseded by another senior general

FACING PAGE: Though staged, this post-battle image shows what the carnage in the Devil's Den looked like. ABOVE LEFT (inset): The Trostle house and barn just days after the battle, showing the destruction wreaked on men and animals alike. ABOVE RIGHT (inset): An artist's rendition of the scene at the Trostle house during the fight. ABOVE: A Reb who gave his all at Gettysburg.

37

BOTTOM: The third day of the battle opened with a scene much like this sketch by battlefield artist A. R. Waud. Troops rushed to the front, while others already there cooked their breakfast and waited for the big fight to come. On the hill crest at left center stands the position that Lee will attack in the grand assault.

RIGHT: The gatehouse of the Evergreen Cemetery on Cemetery Hill, the center of Meade's position, and the object of what would be called Pickett's Charge. It appears here just days after the battle. In fact, the attacking Confederates never reached it, as the painting (far right) might suggest. Still it conveys much of the sense of the scene as reinforcements rushed to assist in repelling the grandest assault of the war in the East. The line of smoke puffs in the distance marks the advance of the attackers, whose battle flags are dimly seen in Edwin Forbes' painting. But no painting could convey the bedlam of sound, smoke, and confusion, attendant to one of the few truly hand-to-hand conflicts of the Civil War.

as fresh troops arrived, but by 3:0 p.m. it looked black for them. Flanked on both sides by Hill's Confederates, with some of Richard Ewell's II Corps veterans now present, the Yankees were finally pushed back into the streets of Gettysburg itself, and beyond, taking up a last line of defense on Cemetery Hill, just south of the town. There they dug in, and there they stayed. They also found General Winfield Scott Hancock there, who now assumed command until Meade could arrive.

The rest of that day and all through the night more units arrived to bolster each army. Lee reached the field that afternoon, and Meade just before dawn on July 2. Looking at the ground, the Federals

ABOVE: One of the older career soldiers who commanded the corps and divisions of the Army of the Potomac was Major General Erasmus D. Keyes, hardly inspired, but competent and dependable. **BELOW:** The tactical importance of Little Round Top is evident in Forbes' painting showing the commanding position that it gave to artillery.

made the best use of the advantage of position. A long, low elevation, Cemetery Ridge, extended southward from Cemetery Hill, and at the southern end sat a tall wooded knob, Little Round Top. More good ground curved eastward away from Cemetery Hill, to Culp's Hill. Meade placed his units along this line, forming the shape of an upside-down fishhook, and decided to stay on the defensive. It was a wise choice.

Lee had studied almost all through the night, talking with his commanders, to decide what to do. He had to attack while Meade's army was incomplete, that much he knew. He finally decided to strike at both ends of the Yankee line simultaneously, with Ewell making a supporting assault on Culp's Hill while Longstreet made the main attack at the opposite end of the Federal position, not far from Little Round Top.

Edwin Forbes left behind many poignant sketches made on the scene, depicting the cost of the battle on large scale and small. For more than an hour before Pickett's Charge, Rebel artillery bombarded the Union lines, seeking to silence its guns. BELOW: This was the aftermath: ruined guns and carriages, and slaughtered animals. Nevertheless, the Yankee artillery emerged relatively unscathed, to pour destruction on the assault.

At first, events seemed to favor Lee. One of Meade's subordinates, General Daniel Sickles, disobeyed his orders and put his III Corps, Meade's left flank, considerably in advance of the line chosen. When Longstreet struck these foolishly exposed troops, he almost destroyed Sickles' corps in an area called the Wheatfield. The battered remnant fell back to the proper line, with the Confederates swinging around and making for Little Round Top. If they took it and put cannon on its crest, they could shell the entire Union line on Cemetery Ridge and force Meade to withdraw. Fortunately, a last

RIGHT: Elon J. Farnsworth never got to wear the stars of a general. Promoted just before the battle, he was killed leading his cavalry brigade in the sideshow cavalry fighting that took place a few miles from the main battlefield on July 3.
FAR RIGHT: A battlefield artist's more finished watercolor sketch of the climactic fighting of July 3. It depicts the moment when the Confederates briefly struck and broke through the Union lines. The officer just going down while holding the flag at left center may be Armistead

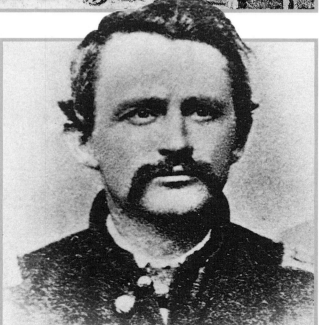

FACING PAGE: On the back slope of Cemetery Ridge, a mute cannon stands where once hundreds repelled the great attack. Meade sits astride "Old Baldy" where he watched the final fury of the battle, and all along the crest monuments proclaim the moment of glory of the Union's sons. **LEFT:** It was a melancholy procession of Confederates who turned their backs to the foe and marched back toward Virginia after the defeat. Forbes left this impression of the Army of Northern Virginia on its retreat toward the Potomac. Nearly a third of their comrades were casualties, and Lee's army would never be entirely the same again.

minute scramble saw Federals get to the summit first and, despite bitter attacks from the foe, the bluecoats held Little Round Top. At the other end of the line, Ewell bungled his Culp's Hill attack.

Meade's line held firm. That night he decided to remain on the defensive, anticipating that Lee's next attack the following day, July 3, would come in the center. He was quite right. Lee, exasperated, could think of nothing else to do. He ordered feints on the flanks of the Federal line, but planned a massive artillery bombardment aimed at the center, on Cemetery Ridge. If he could break through the enemy center, he could roll up either or both halves of the Yankee army.

The bombardment started at 1:0 p.m. and continued for two hours, but most of the shells went wide of their marks, doing no damage. Then Longstreet gave the order for George Pickett's Virginia division and James Pettigrew's North Carolina division to go forward in the grandest frontal assault of the war. "Pickett's Charge," as it would be called, saw the brave Rebels march across a mile of open fields and up into the face of the Yankee rifles and artillery on Cemetery Ridge. It was a doomed effort from the start, but done with incredible gallantry. None broke through, and more than a third never got back.

With the failure of the attack, Lee admitted defeat, and soon started to retreat back toward Virginia. He had lost more than 20,000 of the 70,000 men in his army, while Meade suffered 23,000 out of 90,000. The North was safe, and Lee would never lead another offensive. The tide of the war was turning.

ABOVE: Many of Lee's men – 3,000 of them – would never cross the Potomac again. Like these dead, they lay in rows where they fell or were dragged by the burial parties.

CHAPTER FIVE

ATLANTA

ABOVE: U.S. Grant, the man who planned the road to victory, left the vital task of subduing the enemy army in Georgia to his most able subordinate William T. Sherman (facing page).

Gettysburg was not the only turning point. The day after Lee's defeat, U.S. Grant finally took Vicksburg on the Mississippi. With it he split the Confederacy in two. That fall a Union army took Chattanooga, nearly lost it again after the Battle of Chickamauga, but then survived being besieged to break out and drive the Confederate Army of Tennessee back into north Georgia. That winter Grant was made general-in-chief of all Northern armies, and he set in motion a plan to press the Rebels at all points at once. Meade would advance into Virginia and go after Lee, and the main western armies, led by William Tecumseh Sherman, would go after Atlanta, Georgia, the

South's last major supply and communications center linking the Confederacy east and west. If he could take it, Sherman would split the eastern Confederacy in two.

In early May 1864 Sherman started his campaign, and during the ensuing three months he steadily forced his foe to retreat before him. The Confederate Army of Tennessee, commanded by General Joseph E. Johnston, took a defensive posture from the beginning, in part because it was outnumbered, and in part also because Johnston did not have the moral courage to risk an all-out battle. In a series of engagements – Rocky Face Ridge, Resaca, Cassville, New Hope Church,

BOTTOM (inset): Side-by-side, General Hood's Confederate headquarters sits quietly in the distance, while the foreground reveals newer Federal defenses erected after the Rebels evacuated Atlanta. BELOW (inset): Another view in Atlanta's environs, showing remains of a Confederate fort on Peachtree Street.

FACING PAGE (inset): Another Confederate fort on the Marietta Road, north of Atlanta. Most of these forts never actually saw action, for Hood's attacks in July, and the Battle of Jonesboro weeks later, sealed the city's fate without Sherman having to assault its defenses.

MAIN PICTURE: A dramatic view of the Confederate lines east of Atlanta, showing the ruins of a railroad line, and a locomotive with no cars left to pull. Chimneys show where houses once stood, idle wheels all that remains of boxcars. The scenes of destruction were repeated again and again.

Kennesaw Mountain – Johnston offered only delaying actions, and then withdrew. Only at Kennesaw Mountain did he give Sherman a sound beating, when the Federals unwisely launched precipitate attacks against a well-defended position.

By July Johnston had reached Peachtree Creek, less than five miles from Atlanta itself. By now President Jefferson Davis was exasperated with a general who seemed never to have things sufficiently to his liking to stand and give battle. When Johnston could offer no statement of his plans for defending the city, Davis relieved him of command. Many have since charged Davis with a dreadful mistake in relieving Johnston, but there is no reason to suppose that the general would have done anything but keep retreating if left in charge. Davis' real error, however, was in appointing General John B. Hood as replacement. There was no question of Hood being a bold fighter. He had also intrigued to get the command. But he simply was not smart enough to lead an army.

Fearing that he must act decisively and quickly, Hood ordered an attack just three days after

assuming command. On July 20 he launched the Battle of Peachtree Creek, sending the two corps under Generals William J. Hardee and A.P. Stewart forward to attack George H. Thomas' Army of the Cumberland – one of three so-called armies within Sherman's overall command. Hood hoped to catch Thomas in the open and away from support by other Federal forces. Unfortunately, Thomas proved too stubborn, and Hood proved too weak a manager. The fighting was inconclusive, and when the Confederates withdrew that evening they had suffered casualties almost three times those of the Federals.

But Hood was not to be stopped with one defeat. Two days later he swung Hardee and the corps of Benjamin F. Cheatham around to the east of Atlanta to meet the advancing Federal Army of the Tennessee led by General James McPherson. What followed was the Battle of Atlanta, and once again Hood did not run it well. Cheatham's attack was badly managed and dreadfully late, and when night fell and the Confederates pulled back, they had suffered double the enemy's losses, a fact only redeemed in part by the death of McPherson, the only Yankee

LEFT: An early lithograph offering a melodramatic view of Sherman's "bummers" starting the destruction of Georgia's war materiel. TOP: Sherman's chief of artillery, General William F. Barry, who oversaw much of the neutralization of Confederate works, like those (above) on Peachtree Street in Atlanta.

RIGHT: Two Pennsylvanians who served through the Atlanta Campaign. Brothers, the one at left, Frederick Cordes, fought with the 190th Pennsylvania. Henry, on the right, was in the 18th U.S. Infantry, and lost his left arm at Jonesboro in the last fight before the fall of Atlanta. Both were members of the "Bucktails," Pennsylvania regiments that wore the distinctive deer tail in their hats.

army commander to be killed in battle.

Six days later Hood struck west of Atlanta at McPherson's forces once more, now commanded by General John Schofield. The Battle of Ezra Church only made matters worse. Hood was not on the field – as he had not been during the previous battles – and Schofield's men fought brilliantly. This time Hood's casualties were more than ten times his opponents', and for it he gained nothing. Hood was rapidly destroying his own army.

Throughout August Sherman shelled Atlanta and its defenses, while remaining content not to attack Hood's defenses. Instead, he steadily spread his own lines out, encircling the city and cutting off its railroad communications. By the end of the month, Hood was almost encircled, and tried one last attack, at Jonesboro, twelve miles south of Atlanta, where Sherman threatened to cut the last line. It was another bungled affair, with Hood again absent from the field, and his poor, battered veterans had little fight left in them. The Federals crushed and almost surrounded the Rebels, and took Jonesboro handily. With it gone, all hope of holding Atlanta dissolved, and on September 1 Hood began evacuating the city. "Atlanta is ours," Sherman could wire headquarters,

TOP: The work of destruction of machinery and stores in captured Atlanta commences, as the depots and machinery of the railroad is dismantled or burned.

ABOVE: Boilers, rails, ties, everything related to Confederate transportation, is destroyed.

LEFT: "Sherman's hairpins," they called the twisted iron rails left in the wake of the Yankees' passing. Special tools were made to bend and ruin the red-hot rails, heated over their own burning ties.

CHAPTER SIX

PETERSBURG

The Confederacy was tottering on its knees, everyone could see that. But it was still dangerous. Sherman had not completely crushed Hood. He still had to carry out his March to the Sea to take Savannah and finish splitting the lower South. And even as he occupied Atlanta and sent his victory telegram, his commander, Grant, was facing becoming mired down in one of the longest sieges in history in Virginia.

After Gettysburg, Meade remained in command of the Army of the Potomac, but it would be ten months before it met Lee again in a major contest. The armies feinted through the rest of 1863, then rested and refitted during the winter. In May 1864,

Petersburg was a matter of cannon and fortifications. Batteries like the one at top pounded away at the log and earth works (facing page), while miles of abatis separated the lines.

as Union armies advanced everywhere, Meade moved into an area called the Wilderness, below the Rappahannock, and inaugurated six weeks of almost constant combat, with Grant present in person to supervise. The armies grappled inconclusively through the Wilderness, on to Spotsylvania, then Cold Harbor. By early June Grant and Meade were east of Richmond, roughly where McClellan had been in 1862, but Lee was well entrenched in front of them and could not be budged.

Then Grant conceived the idea of removing his whole army from Lee's front, undetected, and marching south to the James River, crossing over speedily-erected pontoon bridges, then moving a

BELOW: The James River was the greatest geographical obstacle to Union movement, but not great enough to stop Grant, who stole a march on Lee, built a pontoon bridge, and moved his army across it and to the very suburbs of Petersburg before Lee knew what had happened.

few miles west to Petersburg. This city, twenty-five miles south of Richmond, was its key, controlling all but one of the vital rail lines that fed the Confederate Capital. Take Petersburg, and Richmond must fall.

Grant's movement was executed brilliantly. It was almost impossible to fool Lee, but for fully a day Grant left him bewildered, and by June 15 elements

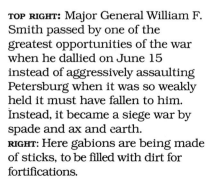

TOP RIGHT: Major General William F. Smith passed by one of the greatest opportunities of the war when he dallied on June 15 instead of aggressively assaulting Petersburg when it was so weakly held it must have fallen to him. Instead, it became a siege war by spade and ax and earth.

RIGHT: Here gabions are being made of sticks, to be filled with dirt for fortifications.

of the Army of the Potomac were on the south side of the James, marching toward a virtually undefended Petersburg. The commander there had but 2,200 men, facing 15,000 in Grant's advance. But that commander was the plucky General Beauregard, hero of Fort Sumter. When the Federals approached, he hastily gathered every spare man, even clerks and shop-keepers, to man his defenses. Then, to Grant's eternal frustration, the Yankee commander on the scene, General W.F. Smith, took his time about attacking, and did not do so until almost dark. If he had moved quickly he could have taken Petersburg. By stalling, he helped prolong the war for another ten months.

Lee sped reinforcements to Petersburg when Beauregard sent word of the threat, and when more determined Yankee attacks came forth on the next and following days, the Rebels managed to repel them. By June 19 Grant realized that all the benefits of his brilliant surprise had been squandered. Lee was ready. There was nothing to do but rest the men after their long campaign, dig earthworks, and commence a siege.

Thus it became a war of spades and shovels for several weeks. With his right anchored on the Appomattox River just to the east of Petersburg, Grant would gradually extend his left below and around the city over the following months, all the

ABOVE: In yet another of Grant's attempts to take the Rebels by surprise, a tunnel was dug between the lines and tons of powder exploded beneath a salient in the Confederate works. The blast created this "crater," into which thousands poured in the unsuccessful attempt to breach the Southern lines.

LEFT: Major General Horatio G. Wright of the VI Corps was one of many Yankee high commanders who suffered the boredom of the siege that followed, with only occasional reassignment for variety.

ABOVE: The attack on the Crater was a fiasco for a number of reasons, not least the timidity of the man sitting at center, General Edward Ferrero. Instead of being with his troops and overseeing their advance after the explosion, he was cowering far in the rear, apparently looking to his own safety first. Nevertheless, he posed confidently with his staff just days after the event, giving no sign that he had ruined his career and cost the lives of hundreds.

RIGHT: Taking a cue from the Yankees, the Rebels, too, commenced tunnels and laying mines. This one was discovered in April 1865 after Petersburg's fall, still incomplete. Called the "Mahone Mine," it, like several others, was evidence of wishful thinking more than concerted tactical planning, and not one Rebel mine was exploded.

while facing a formidable line of defenses erected two years before by the enemy, and now considerably strengthened. There were no battles, and few skirmishes, as the combatants glowered at each other across the lines. Instead, a kind of boredom set in, and the men turned their minds to inventive means of ending the tedium. Thus it was that coal miners in the 48th Pennsylvania Infantry proposed the idea of digging a tunnel from their lines, across to and under the enemy defenses. They would then place a massive charge of gunpowder there, detonate it, and blow a hole in Lee's works, through which the Federals could attack. Grant adopted the idea, in part just to give his men something to do. The work took more than a month, but finally on July 30 all was ready. When the fuze was lit, at first it went out and had to be relit. The resulting explosion blew tens of tons of earth, ramparts, wooden breastworks, cannon, and Confederates, hundreds of feet into the air. But Grant had entrusted the follow-up attack to Generals Ambrose Burnside, James Ledlie,

and Edward Ferrero – a bungler, a drunkard, and a coward respectively. They botched the whole affair, and the result was thousands of casualties and nothing to show for it. Lee held his lines, and the siege went on.

Grant could only keep slowly extending his lines, while making cavalry raids to keep Lee off balance. But the best cavalry raid came from Lee. His cavalry commander, General Wade Hampton, learned that a herd of 2,000 beeves was quartered several miles in rear of Grant's army. In mid-September Hampton sent 4,000 troopers on a daring enterprise to ride clear around the enemy lines and into his rear, to capture the herd and drive it back to Petersburg and its defenders' hungry mouths. It

was a brilliant success that even the Federals had to admire. But it was nothing compared to Grant's steady gains as he cut off one railroad after another. Throughout the fall and into the winter of 1864-5, the Federals continued to lengthen their noose around Lee. There was a score of small engagements, but each ended with the inevitable expansion of Yankee control. Finally, on March 25, Lee authorized a surprise attack calculated to take a key section of the Union works, force Grant to shorten his lines temporarily, and thus allow Lee to get his army and its equipment out of the lines. Petersburg would have to be abandoned, but at least he could save his army. The attack started successfully at first, but it could not sustain its momentum.

TOP: Petersburg, and especially the Crater fiasco, was finally the end of the line for a commander who had been ill-starred throughout the war. Ambrose Burnside had commanded the Army of the Potomac once, but he would be best known to posterity for giving his name to a style of whiskers.
ABOVE LEFT: Reconstructed "bomb proofs" at Petersburg give evidence of soldier wit even in the most trying circumstances, dubbing a rude earth hole the "Willard Hotel."

ABOVE: A. R. Waud's on-the-spot drawing of sharpshooters from the XVIII Corps, coolly firing from their works and picking off Rebels on the other side who were foolish enough to expose themselves.
RIGHT: Jubilant Yankees stand fearlessly atop the works for the first time in April 1865, after the Confederates have pulled out and Petersburg has fallen.

Now it was only a matter of time, and on April 1 the western end of Lee's defensive line collapsed. The Army of Northern Virginia had only hours to get out. On April 2 the evacuation began, a brilliant and desperate rearguard action holding back thousand of attacking Federals while Lee raced westward. Later that same day the Yankees entered Petersburg. The next morning they walked into an undefended Richmond.

The war still had a few weeks to go. One week later Grant brought Lee to bay at Appomattox, where, unable to move in any direction, he was forced to surrender. Sherman had marched to the

RIGHT: The quiet village of Appomattox Courthouse sleeps today as it did in 1865, when the armies came reeling across the Virginia landscape to have their final meeting here, not to make war, but to start the peace. Ironically, Lee and Grant made their terms in the parlor of Wilmer McLean, who had lived alongside Bull Run in 1861, but left to get away from the war. It found him one more time.

BELOW: The ultimate price of the war came in the blood and lives that it cost. This Confederate, killed in the last week of the war at Petersburg, was only one of more than a quarter million Southerners who gave their lives for the cause they espoused. Like these dead (facing page) at Petersburg, they mingled their blood with that of 300,000 Yankee dead, to nurture the soil of a troubled, but reunited, nation.

sea the previous winter, taking Savannah, Georgia in December, then starting a destructive march northward through the Carolinas. Davis had put Johnston back in command of the remnants of the Confederate armies in the region, including the remainder of the Army of Tennessee which Hood had led to near-fatal disaster against Thomas at Nashville in December. But Johnston could do nothing, and he, too, surrendered late in April. With that, the Civil War was virtually over.

Behind them all lay those 10,000 fights, engagements as diverse as an attack on a massive brick fort, iron monsters shooting at each other on the water, lightning virtually striking twice in the same spot called Manassas, the massive conflagration of Gettysburg, a city that became a battleground in Georgia, and the longest siege of the war. It was all a part of the indescribable tragedy of an era when Americans turned the land that they all loved into a battlefield.

CREDITS TO ILLUSTRATIONS

The publishers wish to thank the following individuals and organisations for granting permission to reproduce the illustrations used in this book:

Bettmann Archive; National Archives, Washington, D.C.;
U.S. Army Military Historical Institute, Carlisle, Pennsylvania;
Civil War Times Illustrated, Harrisburg, Pennsylvania;
Western Reserve Historical Society, Cleveland, Ohio; Chicago Historical Society;
Tulane University, New Orleans; Valentine Museum, Richmond, Virginia;
New York Historical Society, New York; The Naval Historical Center;
Minnesota Historical Society; Jon M. Nielson, Orono, Maine;
Alvan Macaulay, Grosse Pointe Farms, Michigan;
National Library of Medicine, Bethesda, Maryland;
Civil War Library and Museum, Philadelphia;
Robert J. Younger, Dayton, Ohio; Wanda Wright, Phoenix, Arizona;
Eugene Wooddell, Waukegan, Illinois; Terence P. O'Leary

ABOVE: **The 73d Ohio Infantry marching off to war from Chillicothe in 1862, a scene repeated all across the country, North and South, as American youth sought adventure.**